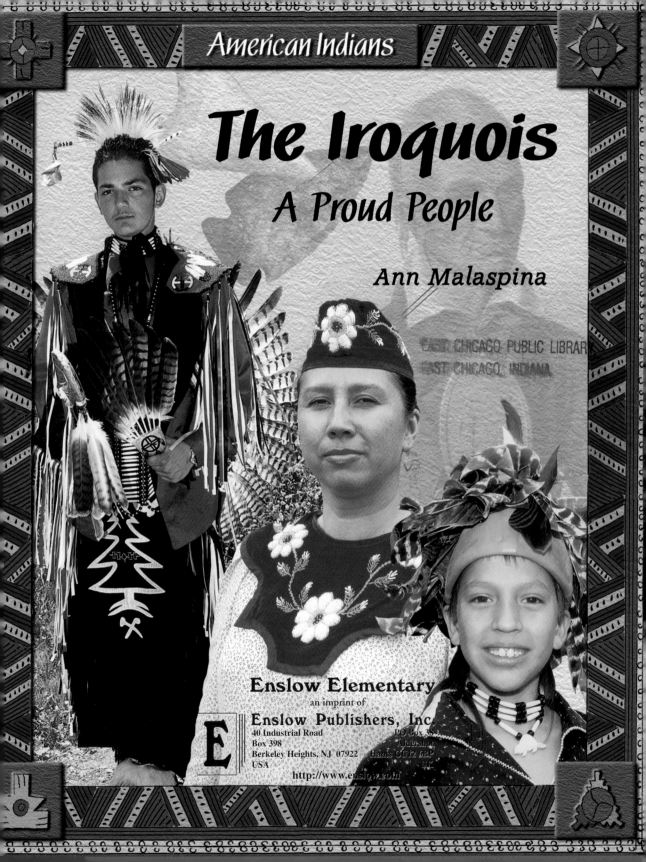

American Indians

The Iroquois
A Proud People

Ann Malaspina

Enslow Elementary
an imprint of

Enslow Publishers, Inc.
40 Industrial Road   PO Box 38
Box 398   Aldershot
Berkeley Heights, NJ 07922   Hants GU12 6BP
USA   UK

http://www.enslow.com

794 3·741

Editor's Note: *We at Enslow Publishers, Inc., are aware that the people of the nation described in this book call themselves Haudenosaunee. However, since they are still often known as the Iroquois, we have decided to use this term. We mean no disrespect to the Haudenosaunee people, but just wish to reach as many readers as possible in order to tell the rich history and current accomplishments of this vibrant people.*

Enslow Elementary, an imprint of Enslow Publishers, Inc.

Enslow Elementary® is a registered trademark of Enslow Publishers, Inc.

Library of Congress Cataloging-in-Publication Data

Malaspina, Ann, 1957–
    The Iroquois : a proud people / Ann Malaspina.
       p. cm. — (American Indians)
    Includes bibliographical references and index.
    ISBN 0-7660-2450-4
    1. Iroquois Indians—History—Juvenile literature. 2. Iroquois Indians—Social life and
customs—Juvenile literature. I. Title. II. Series. III. American Indians (Berkeley Heights, N.J.)
E99.I7M245 2005
974.7004'9755—dc22

            2004016148

To Our Readers: We have done our best to make sure all Internet addresses in this book were active and appropriate when we went to press. However, the author and the publisher have no control over and assume no liability for the material available on those Internet sites or on other Web sites they may link to. Any comments or suggestions can be sent by e-mail to comments@enslow.com or to the address on the back cover.

Illustration Credits: Associated Press/AP, p. 35; Associated Press, THE POST-CRESCENT, p. 40 (bottom); © Bettman/Corbis, p. 22; Clipart.com, pp. 5, 9, 42; © Corel Corporation, pp. 4, 17, 20; © Eastcott-Momatiuk/The Image Works, p. 26; Enslow Publishers, Inc., p. 7; Getty Images, p. 31; © Marilyn "Angel" Wynn, Nativestock.com, pp. 1 (foreground), 14, 15, 16, 23, 28, 29, 32, 43, 44; © Mike Greenlar/The Image Works, p. 34; National Anthropological Archives, p. 18; National Archives of Canada, p. 40 (top); Photos.com, pp. 1 (left background), 13, 19, 24, 27, 33, 37; Reproduced from the Collections of the Library of Congress, pp. 1 (right background), 8, 39; Roberta Jamieson, p. 41; © SSPL/The Image Works, p. 47; © Stock Montage, Inc., pp. 6, 12; © Syracuse Newspapers/David Lassman/The Image Works, p. 21; © Syracuse Newspapers/Albert Fanning/The Image Works, p. 36; © Syracuse Newspapers/Peter Chen/The Image Works, p. 25; Tammy Tarbell-Boehning, p. 30.

Cover Illustration: © Marilyn "Angel" Wynn, Nativestock.com (foreground), Photos.com (left background), Reproduced from the Collections of the Library of Congress (right background).

Contents

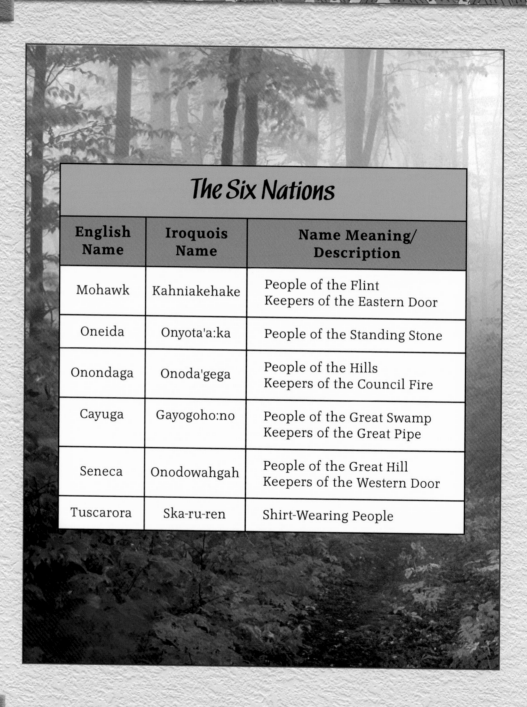

The Six Nations

English Name	Iroquois Name	Name Meaning/ Description
Mohawk	Kahniakehake	People of the Flint Keepers of the Eastern Door
Oneida	Onyota'a:ka	People of the Standing Stone
Onondaga	Onoda'gega	People of the Hills Keepers of the Council Fire
Cayuga	Gayogoho:no	People of the Great Swamp Keepers of the Great Pipe
Seneca	Onodowahgah	People of the Great Hill Keepers of the Western Door
Tuscarora	Ska-ru-ren	Shirt-Wearing People

People of the Longhouse

Long ago, five Iroquois nations—the Mohawk, Oneida, Onondaga, Cayuga, and Seneca—agreed to make peace. For hundreds of years, the League of the Iroquois lived in harmony. The name *Iroquois* came from the French version of a Huron name. It means "black snakes." The Iroquois do not like this name. They called themselves the *Haudenosaunee*, or People of the Longhouse. Their lands crossed the Eastern woodlands like a longhouse. After the Tuscarora joined them in the early 1700s, they became the Six Nations.

Iroquois men were great diplomats. The women chose the chiefs. Iroquois children learned ways of their ancestors. Great changes swept across their lands. Yet the Haudenosaunee's beliefs and traditions lived on.

chapter one

The Land

"There was a time when our forefathers owned this great island," said Seneca Chief Red Jacket in 1805. Then the settlers came. Red Jacket then said, "Brother: Our seats were once large, and yours were small. You have now become a great people, and we have scarcely a place left to spread our blankets."

The Iroquois Then

The Iroquois territory stretched from the Hudson River to Lake Erie and south from Lake Ontario in what is now upstate New York. By the 1600s, Iroquois hunters stalked deer as far away as Kentucky and Ohio. But European settlers soon arrived.

The Iroquois lived in villages of long houses.

Most Iroquois villages were in New York. The main areas where they lived are shown by the group names in purple. The orange squares show where some of the present-day Iroquois reservations are. During the 1600s, the Iroquois controlled most of the northeastern United States and eastern Canada.

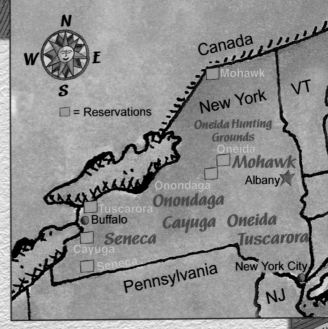

After the Revolutionary War, the Iroquois were forced to sell the land for less than it was worth. Much later, the United States took more land for reservoirs and power plants.

The Iroquois Today

Today, Iroquois reservations are in Ontario, Quebec, New York, Wisconsin, and Oklahoma. The Six Nations of the Grand River Reserve in Ontario covers about forty-five thousand acres. Families also live in cities in the United States and Canada. No matter how far away they live, the Iroquois care about their land and often return for visits.

❖ chapter two ❖

History

Early Iroquois probably migrated to New York about six thousand years ago. As time passed, they separated into nations, but soon the nations were at war.

The Peacemaker

Sometime before the 1500s, Deganawidah brought peace to his people. He was called the Peacemaker. He and his helper, Hiawatha, persuaded the chiefs to put down their weapons. The chiefs planted a white pine tree to show unity. "Roots have spread out from the Tree of the Great Peace, one to the north, one to the east, one to the south and

In this painting, Hiawatha waves goodbye to his people from a canoe.

one to the west. The name of these roots is The Great White Roots and their nature is Peace and Strength," said Deganawidah. He recited the Great Law of Peace, the rules for the new confederacy, or government of the Iroquois.

In the early 1600s, European fur traders came from Quebec and up the Hudson River. It was not easy to share the land. In 1609, the French explorer Samuel de Champlain killed several Mohawk warriors. The Iroquois made peace with the British in 1692. However, the old life was disappearing. In 1634, a disease called smallpox killed many Mohawks. Diseases brought by settlers killed over half the Iroquois.

The Tuscarora fled North Carolina and joined the Confederacy in 1722. The Iroquois grew stronger and defeated the Hurons. The Iroquois became the most

Champlain fought the Iroquois with guns and the help of other American Indians.

powerful group of American Indians east of the Mississippi River.

The American Revolution (1775–1783)

During the Revolutionary War, the Oneida and Tuscarora fought with the colonists. Other Iroquois fought with the British. All Iroquois suffered. In 1779, General George Washington's soldiers burned forty Iroquois villages, fields, and orchards. "Indians were hired to fight against

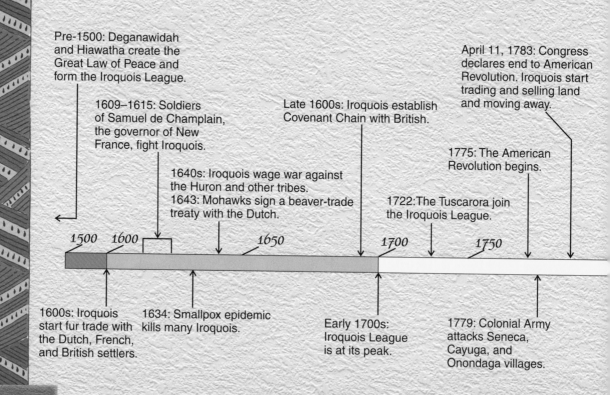

Pre-1500: Deganawidah and Hiawatha create the Great Law of Peace and form the Iroquois League.

1609–1615: Soldiers of Samuel de Champlain, the governor of New France, fight Iroquois.

Late 1600s: Iroquois establish Covenant Chain with British.

April 11, 1783: Congress declares end to American Revolution. Iroquois start trading and selling land and moving away.

1775: The American Revolution begins.

1640s: Iroquois wage war against the Huron and other tribes.
1643: Mohawks sign a beaver-trade treaty with the Dutch.

1722:The Tuscarora join the Iroquois League.

1500   1600   1650   1700   1750

1600s: Iroquois start fur trade with the Dutch, French, and British settlers.

1634: Smallpox epidemic kills many Iroquois.

Early 1700s: Iroquois League is at its peak.

1779: Colonial Army attacks Seneca, Cayuga, and Onondaga villages.

Indians, and many of our people were destroyed," said Red Jacket, a Seneca chief.

The war ended in 1783. The colonists had won. But the Iroquois lost most of their land. Many Iroquois moved to Canada. Others settled in Wisconsin and Oklahoma. The Six Nations were almost destroyed. In 1794, the Iroquois won sovereignty in the Treaty of Canandaigua. It meant the Iroquois were independent with a right to some of their original land.

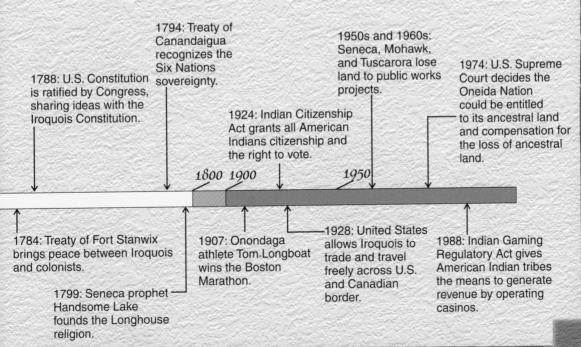

1794: Treaty of Canandaigua recognizes the Six Nations sovereignty.

1788: U.S. Constitution is ratified by Congress, sharing ideas with the Iroquois Constitution.

1950s and 1960s: Seneca, Mohawk, and Tuscarora lose land to public works projects.

1974: U.S. Supreme Court decides the Oneida Nation could be entitled to its ancestral land and compensation for the loss of ancestral land.

1924: Indian Citizenship Act grants all American Indians citizenship and the right to vote.

1800   1900   1950

1784: Treaty of Fort Stanwix brings peace between Iroquois and colonists.

1907: Onondaga athlete Tom Longboat wins the Boston Marathon.

1928: United States allows Iroquois to trade and travel freely across U.S. and Canadian border.

1988: Indian Gaming Regulatory Act gives American Indian tribes the means to generate revenue by operating casinos.

1799: Seneca prophet Handsome Lake founds the Longhouse religion.

chapter three

Homes

The Iroquois settled on hills near a river or lake. The men built palisades, or wooden stake fences, around a group of longhouses. Palisades kept out enemies and wild animals. Outside the palisades lay fields of corn, beans, and squash.

The Iroquois Then

The longhouse frame was made of white cedar logs and covered with elm bark. The building might be 20 feet wide and 40 to 200 feet long. Doors stood at both ends.

The frame of a longhouse was built first. Then it was covered with bark.

An arched roof kept the snow off. On the longhouse doors hung a bear, turtle, or other clan symbol.

Many families of the same clan lived in a longhouse. Clans are extended families that share a female ancestor. Families slept on wooden platforms covered with cornhusk mats and furs. Tools, baskets, and clothes were stored in high platforms. Cooking fires burned along the central walkway.

The Iroquois Today

Today, the nations' longhouses are used for religious and community meetings. Most families live in houses, apartments, and mobile homes. New townhouses were built in the 1990s at the Oneida Indian Nation in Central New York. Children and elders gather at the recreation center nearby, built in the shape of a longhouse.

Today, the Iroquois live in all types of homes.

13

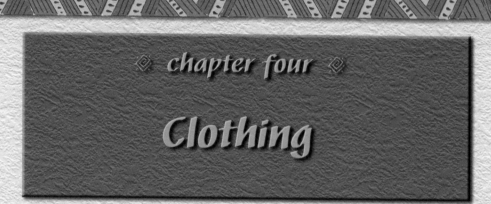

❖ chapter four ❖

Clothing

Iroquois clothes were made of deerskin. The Iroquois traded beaver pelts for colorful glass beads. Women stitched the beads into pretty patterns on dresses and moccasins. Traditional clothes are worn today for celebrations.

The Iroquois Then

In winter, men wore loincloths, fringed shirts, and leggings. Women wore dresses and leggings, perhaps with a fancy belt or silver ornament. Moccasins were made from deer, elk, or moose. Snowshoes allowed them to walk in the forest. Bear fur robes

This boy wears a traditional kastoweh.

Until an Iroquois girl is married, she wears her hair in two braids. After she is married, a woman wears only one braid.

kept the wind out. After Europeans traded cloth to the Iroquois, the men wore sashes decorated with quills and beads. Women began sewing clothes from cloth.

Some men shaved their hair in a crest, called a scalp lock. They wore a feathered hat called a kastoweh. The eagle feathers on top represented the man's nation. Married women wore their hair in a single braid. Young girls wore two braids.

The Iroquois Today

Today, Iroquois teenagers dress in the latest fashions. Traditional clothes are for special occasions. At the Oneida's annual celebration, a girl's dress might be embroidered with beads in lovely designs such as a clan symbol, flowers, or a strawberry.

chapter five

Food and Meals

Families shared the morning meal every day. Then they ate a little when they were hungry. A tasty soup or stew was always ready if guests stopped by.

The Iroquois Then

The Iroquois relied on the natural world for food. They tapped maple trees for sweet syrup. They also picked wild blackberries in the summer. They were expert farmers. The most important foods were corn, beans, and squash, or the Three Sisters. The seeds were planted together on small hills. Corn stalks supported the climbing

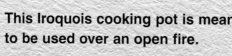

This Iroquois cooking pot is meant to be used over an open fire.

Corn and squash are an important part of the Iroquois diet. The Iroquois also use special types of squash called gourds to make bowls and musical instruments.

beans. Squash vines helped trap moisture to feed the crops. The Iroquois believed the Three Sisters were a gift from the Creator. The women boiled, roasted, or baked the food in clay pots in the fire pits.

The Iroquois Today

Today, Iroquois eat a typical American diet. They shop in supermarkets and eat out in restaurants. They try to eat balanced diets to avoid diseases like high blood pressure, obesity, and diabetes. Tribal health officials encourage healthy, low-fat food. The Oneida Nation published the *Three Sisters Cookbook* in 1994. It has delicious recipes for corn, squash, and beans.

chapter six

Family Life

Every family member works hard. Children help with chores. Elders give advice. Aunts, uncles, nieces, nephews, and cousins are important, too. This circle of community is the Iroquois way of life.

The Iroquois Then

Each Iroquois belonged to one of nine clans—Deer, Bear, Wolf, Hawk, Snipe, Heron, Beaver, Eel, or Turtle. Each clan was led by the wise clan mother. A baby was born into its mother's clan. One could not marry someone in his or her clan, and men joined their wives' clans.

Women held a lot of power. They owned the land and longhouses. They decided when

This Iroquois woman holds her baby in a cradleboard. The strong wood of the cradleboard helps support the baby's neck.

Furs helped the Iroquois keep warm during the winter.

to go to war. The men hunted and defended the people. They protected their clans in times of danger. They cut the logs for the longhouse and provided fur for the winter robes.

The Iroquois Today

Today, Iroquois men and women share responsibilities. Both parents may work outside the home. They also care for homes and families. Iroquois still belong to clans. The clans keep the circle of the community alive.

Many Iroquois marry in Christian churches. Others have an Iroquois wedding in the longhouse. The man and woman exchange wedding baskets. The new husband and wife share a white corn wedding cake and dance the sacred Great Feather Dance.

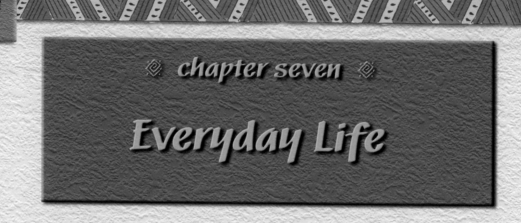

chapter seven ◈

Everyday Life

The Iroquois have always honored the family while engaging in the duties of daily life.

The Iroquois Then

Every morning when they awoke, the Iroquois said a Thanksgiving Prayer to the Creator. The women lit the longhouse fires. They prepared corn-and-beans stew and roasted corn cakes over the fire.

In late summer, the women gathered corn from the fields. Girls helped weave baskets and sleeping mats from corn stalks. They dug up clay to make cooking pots. They also soaked deer hide to soften it for making dresses.

The Iroquois needed patience and courage to hunt the dangerous black bear of the Northeast.

This Iroquois man teaches two children how to play a traditional drum.

After the age of eight or nine, the boys joined their fathers and uncles. They were taught how to use a bow and arrow, make an axe with wood and flint, and cut trees to clear fields.

When the autumn leaves fell, the men came home from the hunt with bear, turkey, deer, rabbit, and other game. The women dried the meat for winter. They scraped and pounded the skin for clothes. The men carved the bones into fishing hooks.

In quiet times, the women wove black ash baskets to store dried beans. The men repaired the longhouse roof for winter. The girls made corn husk dolls. Outside, the boys wrestled and raced each other.

When winter came, Iroquois filled baskets with cornmeal. Dried fish hung from rafters. At night, the elders told stories. Some were about ghosts and monsters. Every story had a special meaning.

The Iroquois Today

Iroquois own businesses, work as policemen, and write for newspapers. They teach in universities and practice law. They are nurses and doctors. Since the 1880s, many Mohawk have worked as ironworkers or "skywalkers." They climb dangerously high beams to build skyscrapers and bridges.

Tuscarora children in Lewiston, New York, learn their history and culture at the Tuscarora school. They also learn the Tuscarora language, called *Skarure*. Recently, fifth graders interviewed elders about hunting and fishing. They recorded the Tuscarora

Iroquois "skywalkers" work on very tall buildings. Here, Bob Snow works high above New York City!

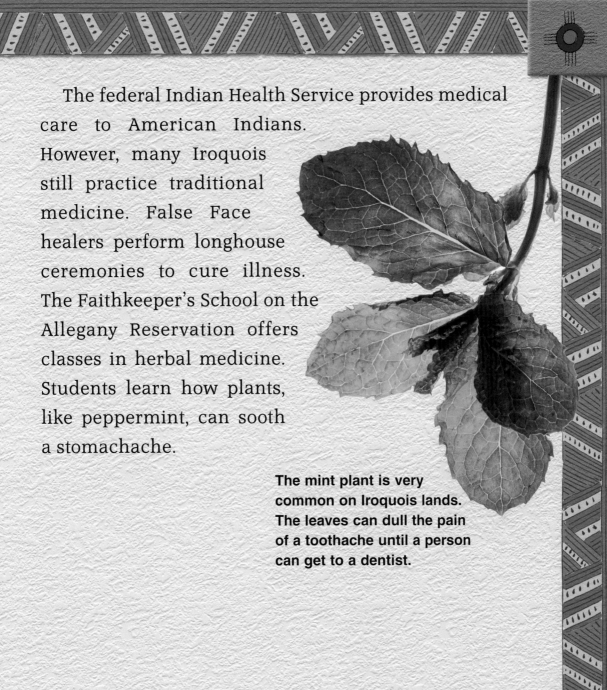

The federal Indian Health Service provides medical care to American Indians. However, many Iroquois still practice traditional medicine. False Face healers perform longhouse ceremonies to cure illness. The Faithkeeper's School on the Allegany Reservation offers classes in herbal medicine. Students learn how plants, like peppermint, can sooth a stomachache.

The mint plant is very common on Iroquois lands. The leaves can dull the pain of a toothache until a person can get to a dentist.

chapter nine

Art and Music

Art and music were woven into everyday life for the Iroquois. Young boys learned to play the wooden flute or beat rhythms on a water drum. Girls carved beautiful designs on ordinary clay pots. They wove special patterns into baskets used to carry corn and beans.

The Iroquois Then

Singing and dancing filled the longhouse during an Iroquois ceremony. The beating of the water drum was like the heartbeat of Mother Earth. Social dances like the Robin Dance, the Duck Dance, and the Alligator Dance were performed for celebrations.

Iroquois of all ages perform in social dances.

This rattle was made from a turtle shell by a Seneca.

The Great Feather Dance was performed only for the most sacred ceremonies.

During sacred ceremonies, shamans shook turtle-shell rattles. The rattles were made from the shells of snapping turtles, box turtles, and mud turtles. They were filled with small pebbles, corn kernels, or fruit pits. The handle was made from wood splints and wrapped in animal skin. A turtle's head was tied at the end. Like wampum and False Face masks, turtle rattles are sacred and should not be displayed in museums or traded or sold.

The Iroquois Today

Iroquois artists are busy today. At the New York State Museum, Iroquois artists display beadwork, gourd rattles, embroidered pincushions, and stone sculpture. Iroquois baskets are especially admired. The basket makers on the St. Regis Mohawk Reservation still gather

Tammy Tarbell-Boehning displays a ceramic pot in her studio.

the grasses and weave beautiful sweet grass and black ash splint baskets. Geometric patterns make each basket one of a kind.

Fine artists work in watercolor, oil, clay, and silver. Mohawk sculptor Tammy Tarbell-Boehning creates clay figures of American Indian women. She studied ceramics in college and has won many awards. Her work has been displayed at the Smithsonian Museum of the American Indian and other museums. One of her works, "Grandmother Moon," is the great Iroquois spirit seen in the face of a woman.

Iroquois musicians perform around the world. Oneida singer and songwriter Joanne Shenandoah, a Wolf Clan member, weaves ancient music into popular songs. "Most of my songs are written with messages of love, peace and hope," said Shenandoah. Her songs are based on Iroquois myths and history. Her 2003 album, *Covenant*, was named for the Iroquois word for very important agreements made between people. In the opening song, "Giving Thanks," Mohawk Chief Jake Swamp recites the Thanksgiving Prayer. Joanne's music plays in the background.

Joanne Shenandoah performs at the World Music Celebration on June 17, 2000 in New Mexico. The singer and songwriter has been nominated for a Grammy award.

chapter ten

Sports and Games

The Iroquois enjoyed games and sports. Games were a way to make friends and learn to work together. Sports helped the Iroquois develop speed and strength. Games taught young people hunting skills, like stalking, and fighting skills, like attacking.

Onondaga boys pose with their lacrosse sticks in Howes Cave, New York.

The Iroquois Then

Lacrosse was a very popular Iroquois sport. The men played lacrosse on a long field. Players carried a wooden stick with a net. They ran down the field, passing the ball. The ball was made of wood, baked clay, or stone. Players tried to shoot the ball past the goal posts. Hundreds of players competed. The game could last for days.

The Iroquois believed the Creator gave them the game as a gift. They thought lacrosse was a "medicine game" that could heal sickness. Players prayed and fasted before a game. They burned tobacco to give thanks.

In winter, the Iroquois played snow snake. They used flexible hickory sticks shaped like snakes. The sticks were polished smooth. Players dragged a log through a snow bank to make an icy track. Players got a running start and threw the stick. The man who slithered his stick the farthest was the winner.

The Iroquois liked games of chance. During the Midwinter Festival, they played the Bowl Game. They used fruit pits for dice. The pits were colored black on one side. Players took turns throwing the dice into a wooden bowl. The player with the most dice showing the black side won the game.

Peach pits were often used to play the Bowl Game. In order to get the playing pieces, Iroquois boys and girls got to enjoy a healthy snack.

The Iroquois Today

Today, Iroquois boys and girls enjoy many sports. They play ice hockey, basketball, football, baseball, softball, and they figure skate. Athletes compete at all levels, including professional hockey and lacrosse.

Modern lacrosse is played by both boys and girls. Tribal teams, like the Oneida Silverhawks, compete in the Iroquois Lacrosse Association. The best players of the Six Nations join the Iroquois Nationals Lacrosse Team. This is the only American Indian team to compete around the world. The Iroquois Nationals won the bronze medal in the 1999 World Championships in Adelaide, Australia.

The Iroquois Nationals lacrosse team poses for a photo.

Today, lacrosse is enjoyed by boys, girls, men, and women. There are Iroquois on teams at both the college and professional level. Even people who are not Iroquois enjoy the game.

Snow snake contests are held today in New York and Ontario. Players carve designs on their snow-snake sticks. They have tricks to make their snake go the fastest and farthest. They keep the tricks secret from all the other players. The thrower who is strongest and most accurate usually wins the snow-snake competition.

chapter eleven

Warfare

Iroquois men were famous for their courage in war. They fought for hunting rights and to defend their people. When the Europeans came, the Iroquois defended their land and, later, fought bravely in the American Revolution. Then they put down their weapons and signed peace treaties.

The Iroquois Then

The Iroquois carved arrowheads from stones. Bows were made of hickory, ash, oak, or cedar wood. A stone attached to a wooden handle was the Iroquois war club.

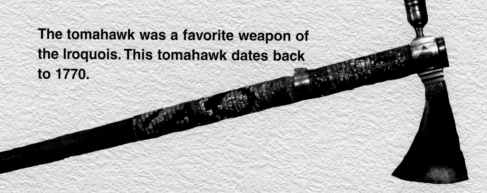

The tomahawk was a favorite weapon of the Iroquois. This tomahawk dates back to 1770.

The club was deadly when thrown at the enemy. Shields were covered with animal hide. In 1648, the Dutch sold four hundred guns to the Iroquois Nation. Later, the Iroquois traded with settlers for guns.

Arrowheads were made from stone. They are still found in people's backyards today.

The Iroquois Today

Today, the Iroquois go to court to recover their land and protect their rights. The Cayuga filed suit in 1980 to reclaim the land near Cayuga Lake. A federal judge ruled in 2003 that the land should be returned to the Cayuga.

Iroquois serve in all branches of the U.S. military. They fought in World War I, World War II, and in Iraq. "We are warriors from way back," said George Heron, a Seneca leader and World War II Navy veteran.

chapter twelve

Heroes

The European settlers called the Iroquois chiefs "forest diplomats." They respected the Iroquois leaders because they treated people fairly. Through the years, Iroquois men and women have become part of United States history.

The Iroquois Then

Joseph Brant, a Mohawk born in 1742, was a brilliant soldier and leader. He led the Mohawk, Seneca, Cayuga, and Onondaga on the side of the British during the American Revolution. He feared the Iroquois would lose their land if the colonists won. After the British lost the war, he led the Iroquois to a reservation in Ontario. The City of Brantford, Ontario, is named for Brant's role in building Canada.

Red Jacket, the Seneca chief, got his English name because he wore the British red coat during the

American Revolution. He was a great diplomat. After the war, he made peace with the new United States. George Washington, the first president, gave him a silver medal of peace in 1792. Red Jacket wanted to preserve Iroquois customs and religion.

Ely Samuel Parker, a Seneca, was a general for the Union Army of the North during the Civil War. He wrote the terms of

Red Jacket was a Seneca chief. He served as official spokesman for the whole Iroquois Confederacy for a time.

surrender for General Robert E. Lee to sign in 1865. Later, he was the first American Indian to serve as the Commissioner of Indian Affairs in Washington, D.C.

The Iroquois Today

Onondaga athlete Tom Longboat won the Boston Marathon in 1907. He set a new record with his time of 2 hours, 24 minutes.

Tom Longboat came from Canada to win the Boston Marathon. A marathon is a race that lasts for 26 miles 385 yards.

Clinton Rickard, a Tuscarora chief, led a protest of the 1924 Immigration Act, which forbade Iroquois from entering the United States or Canada without passports. Iroquois are now allowed to freely cross the border. Rickard founded the Indian Defense League of America. The group fights injustice against American Indians.

Actor Graham Greene, an Oneida, was born on the Six Nations Reserve. He has often portrayed American Indians in

Oneida actor Graham Greene introduces some other actors at an acting class in Wisconsin. Greene hopes to start American Indian theater groups in the United States.

films. He was nominated for an Oscar for Best Supporting Actor for his role in the 1990 film *Dances with Wolves* with Kevin Costner.

In 1976, Roberta Jamieson was the first Canadian Indian woman in Canada to earn a law degree. She was appointed commissioner of the Indian Commission of Ontario in 1986. In 2001, Jamieson became the first woman to be elected chief of the Six Nations Reserve.

Roberta Jamieson is a great Iroquois chief.

chapter thirteen

Government

The Iroquois Confederacy is the oldest democracy in the world. "We were instructed to create societies based on the principles of Peace, Equity, Justice, and the Power of Good Minds," says Onondaga Faithkeeper Oren Lyons.

The Iroquois Then

The Great Law spelled out how chiefs are chosen and gave women and men equal rights. It told how land was owned and arguments were settled. Chiefs, chosen by clan mothers, led the people. The nations sent fifty chiefs to the Grand Council at the Onondaga Nation. They made

This Iroquois chief was was picked by his group's clan mothers. His kastoweh shows how important he is.

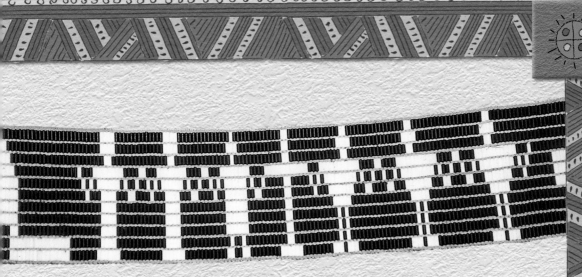

Important laws were recorded on wampum belts.

decisions about war, peace, and treaties for all Iroquois. Decisions had to be agreed upon by everyone. Important treaties and laws were recorded on wampum belts.

America's Founders respected the ideas in the Iroquois' laws. The U.S. Constitution and the Great Law share many ideas about a person's rights and freedoms.

The Iroquois Today

The Iroquois nations still govern themselves. Iroquois chiefs meet every year for the Grand Council. The central fire still burns at the Onondaga Nation, as it did when the Peacekeeper recited the Great Law.

The Seventh Generation

The Iroquois look ahead to the Seventh Generation, or the children yet to be born. "When we walk upon Mother Earth, we always plant our feet carefully because we know the faces of our future generations are looking up at us from beneath the ground," says Oren Lyons, Turtle Clan Faithkeeper of the Onondaga Nation of the Iroquois.

The Iroquois celebrate their culture every day. Seneca Lehman Dowdy says, "Now it is time to teach our children the language and the culture so this knowledge will carry on forever."

Lyons has great hope for the future of her people: "As long as there's one to sing and one to dance, one to speak and one to listen, life will go on."

Words to Know

breechcloth—Deerskin or cloth fabric worn as a covering.

clan—A social and family group sharing a common female ancestor. The nine Iroquois clans are Deer, Bear, Wolf, Hawk, Snipe, Heron, Beaver, Eel, and Turtle.

confederacy—The union of the six Iroquois nations under one set of laws.

council—The ruling bodies of the Iroquois clan, nation, and confederacy.

Faithkeeper—Spiritual leader who preserves and passes on beliefs of the Iroquois.

kastoweh—Feathered hat worn by Iroquois men.

longhouse—Traditional shelter of the Iroquois made from wood and bark.

reservation—Area of land reserved for tribes, created by treaties, acts of Congress, or executive order or agreement. In Canada, known as reserves.

sachem—Respected Iroquois chief, chosen by the clan mother.

shaman—Iroquois medicine man or healer.

Three Sisters—Corn, beans, and squash.

wampum—Purple and white beads woven in designs to record events, treaties, and laws.

Bruchac, Joseph, editor. *The Boy who Lived with Bears and Other Iroquois Stories*. New York: HarperCollins, 1995.

Bruchac, Joseph. *Eagle Song*. New York: Dial Books for Young Readers, 1997.

Favor, Lesli J. *The Iroquois Constitution*. New York: Rosen Publishing Group, 2003.

Levine, Ellen. *If You Lived with The Iroquois*. New York: Scholastic, 1998.

Ridington, Jillian and Robin. *People of the Longhouse*. Buffalo, N.Y.: Firefly Books, 1995.

Shenandoah, Joanne. *Skywoman: Legends of the Iroquois*. Sante Fe: Clear Light Publishers, 1998.

Zabol, Myron and Lorre Jensen. *People of the Dancing Sky: The Iroquois Way*. New York: St. Martin's Press, 2000.

Internet Addresses

Haudenosaunee: People Building a Long House

<http://www.sixnations.org>

Iroquois Indian Museum

<http://www.iroquoismuseum.org>

Oneida Indian Nation

<http://www.oneida_nation.net/>

The Iroquois game of lacrosse

Index